LEARN TO DRAW

DISNEY · PIXAR

CHARACTERS

*Featuring Woody, Buzz Lightyear, Lightning McQueen,
Mater, and other favorite characters*

Illustrated by the Disney Storybook Artists

Walter Foster

1 3 5 7 9 10 8 6 4 2

Table of Contents

Tools & Materials. 4

Getting Started. 5

Carl Fredricksen 6

Russell. 10

Carl's House. 14

Kevin. 16

Dug. 18

Merida 20

Elinor the Bear. 24

Woody 28

Buzz Lightyear 30

Lightning McQueen 32

Mater 34

WALL-E 36

EVE. 38

Nemo 40

Dory 42

Sulley 44

Mike 46

Boo 48

Remy. 50

Linguini & Remy 52

Mr. Incredible 54

Elastigirl 56

Frozone 58

Flik 60

Atta 62

The End 64

Tools & Materials

Ready, set, go! Lightning McQueen may require some fancy tools
for a tune-up, but all you need to start drawing him—and all of his friends—
are a few supplies. Use a pencil to get your drawing engine running.
Then you can add color with felt-tip markers, colored pencils,
watercolors, or acrylic paints.

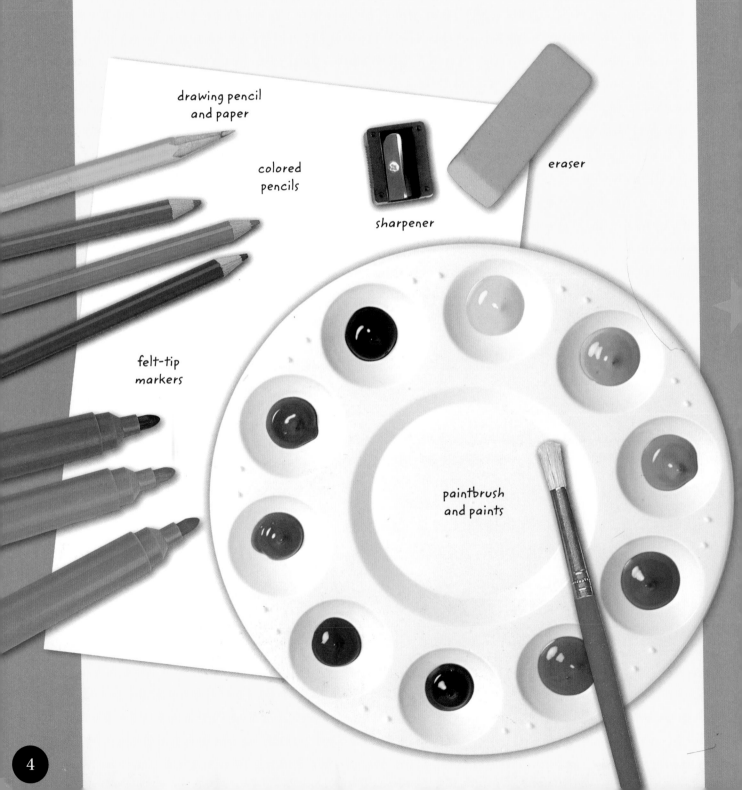

drawing pencil
and paper

colored
pencils

sharpener

eraser

felt-tip
markers

paintbrush
and paints

Getting Started

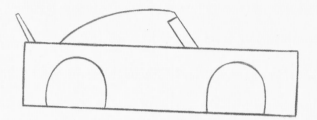

Step 1

First draw the basic shapes.

Step 2

Each new step is shown in blue.

Step 3

Follow the blue lines to add the details.

Step 4

Now darken the lines you want to keep and erase the rest.

Add color!

Carl Fredricksen

Carl Fredricksen is a shy 78 year old who wishes people would leave him alone. Each morning Carl meticulously vacuums every surface and straightens every doily, making sure things are just as his beloved late wife, Ellie, left them. After his morning cleaning ritual, Carl eats the same breakfast he's eaten every day for the past 50 years. Then he puts on his hat, sits on his porch, and glares at people talking too loudly into their newfangled portable phones as they walk by.

Carl's body is blocky, and his head is square shaped

1

2

hair is divided into 3 sections

large   medium   small

NO!

YES!

without the glasses, Carl's
eyes are neutral — not mad

3

4

fingers are blocky

start with square glasses

cut in for nose

5

6

Carl is about 2 heads tall

Russell

Russell is Carl Fredricksen's neighbor. He has enough gear to make him the most prepared 8-year-old Junior Wilderness Explorer in Explorer history. The only problem is, he's never been anywhere except the Camping Museum downtown. Determined to get his "Assisting the Elderly" badge and be promoted to Senior Wilderness Explorer, Russell's dream is to attend the father-son ceremony so his dad can pin on Russell's new badge. First, Russell must hound Carl Fredricksen with assistance—even if it means following Carl to the ends of the globe and back.

body is roughly egg shaped

1

2

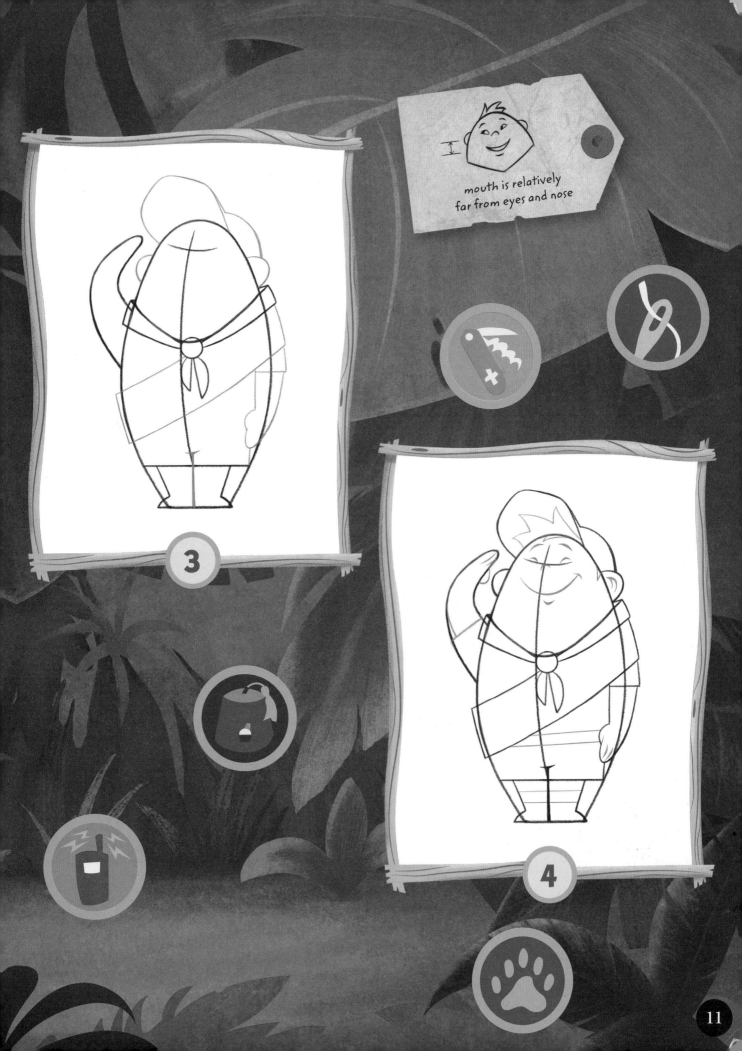

mouth is relatively
far from eyes and nose

3

4

start with simple flipper-like arms; then add fingers

5

6

12

Carl's House

Carl loves the home he shared with Ellie because it is filled with many happy memories of their life together. When Carl is ordered out of his house, he seizes the opportunity to fulfill Ellie's lifelong dream of living at Paradise Falls in South America. Carl ties thousands of balloons to his house, climbs inside, and escapes up into the clouds on an exciting adventure!

Square objects represent Carl; round objects represent Ellie. The roof has a blend of shapes to show that the house is a part of both of them.

4

5

6

Only draw a few bricks on the chimney. It's easier and has the same effect!

Kevin

Named by Russell, Kevin is a 12-foot-tall flightless jungle bird whom Russell sets free from a trap. Forever grateful, Kevin—a female—follows Russell and Carl on their adventure.

eyes stare straight out—they do not point in a specific direction

YES!

NO!

Kevin is big compared to Carl and Russell

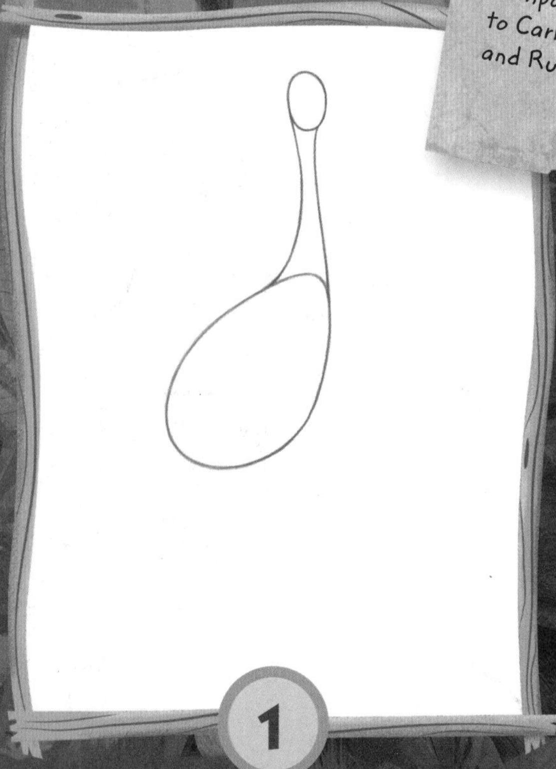

feather patterns are irregular

NO!

YES!

1

2

3

to look down, she turns her head in funny angles

4

6

5

head feather has a bulb-like end

Dug

Dug is a desperate dog who wants nothing more than to be part of a pack. Because of a technological invention, Dug can verbally communicate with humans. Unfortunately, this talking device doesn't help Dug much in the "brains" department, but he'll do anything to make his master happy. Dug must decide who deserves his loyalty—the pack he's known his entire life or this new pack with Carl and Russell.

nose swoops up

1

2

body is pudgy and rounded

NO!   YES!

3

4

6

5

tail fur
flares
most
in the
middle

paws are small
compared to body

MERIDA

Merida is the adventurous Princess of DunBroch. More comfortable in the woods with her bow than in a ball gown, Merida would be perfectly content to ride her horse, Angus, around all day in the sunshine.

6

for Merida's
hair, use wild,
squiggly lines

7

eyes and brow
are more round

NO!   YES!

ELINOR THE BEAR

Elinor is transformed into a bear when she eats a cake that the Witch gave to Merida.
Merida and Elinor the Bear embark on a journey to find the Witch to change Elinor back,
and in the process, mother and daughter grow closer than ever.

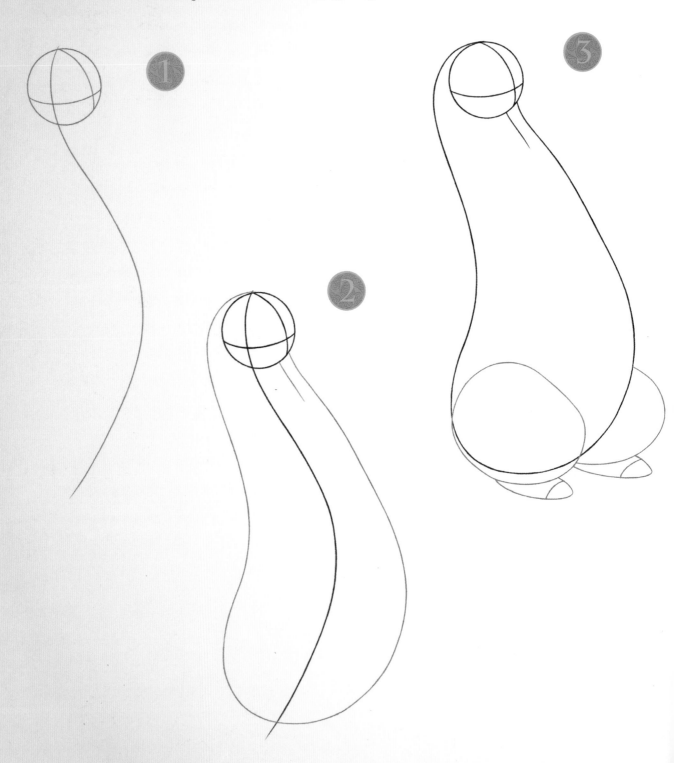

NO! not spaced
too evenly

YES! five claws
grouped
together

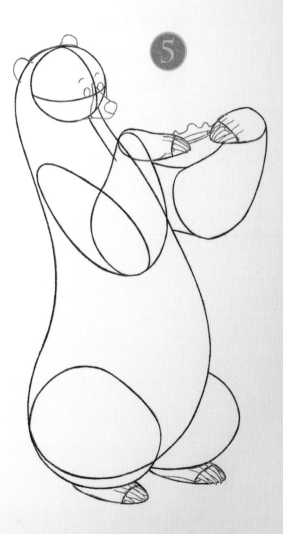

6

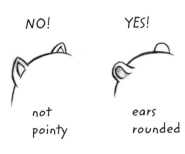

NO!   YES!

not
pointy

ears
rounded

no cartoon-like
eyes

7

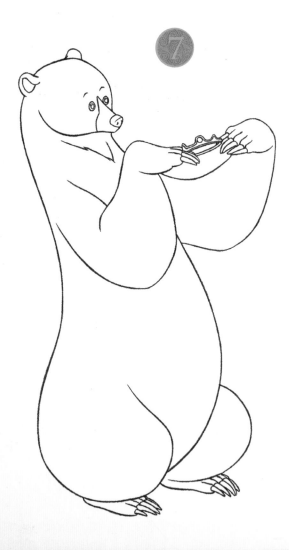

WOODY

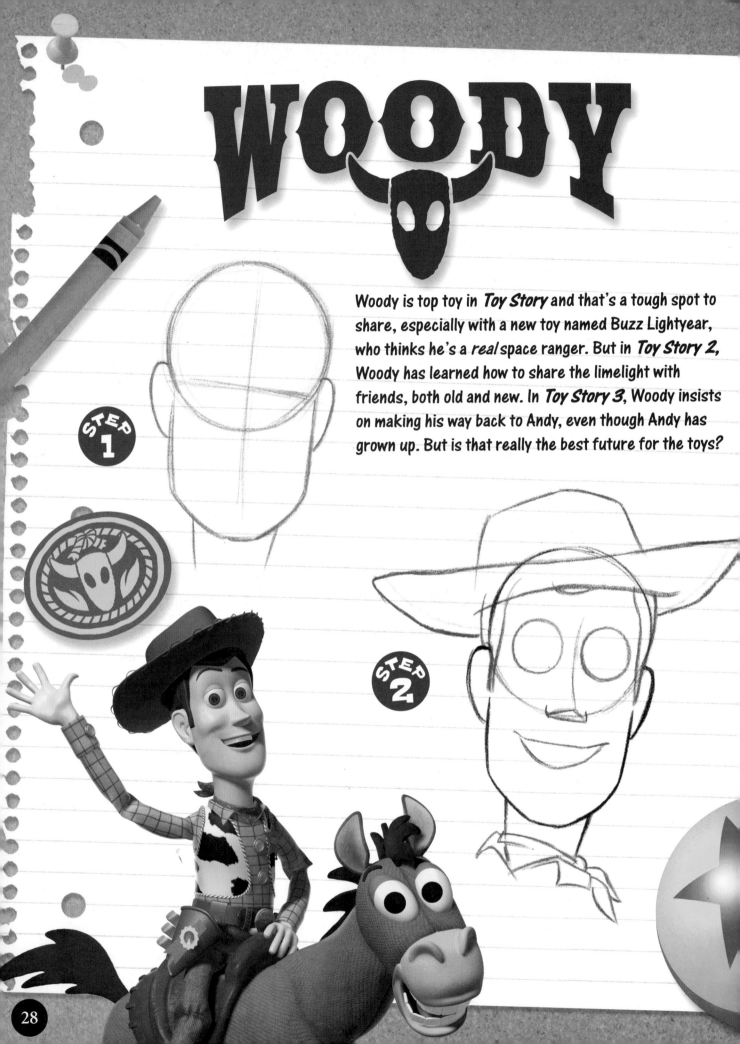

Woody is top toy in *Toy Story* and that's a tough spot to share, especially with a new toy named Buzz Lightyear, who thinks he's a *real* space ranger. But in *Toy Story 2,* Woody has learned how to share the limelight with friends, both old and new. In *Toy Story 3*, Woody insists on making his way back to Andy, even though Andy has grown up. But is that really the best future for the toys?

STEP 1

STEP 2

round eyes

large iris

ears are flat
on top

STEP 3

YES!

NO!
too
straight

YES!
teeth are one long
rectangle

NO!

Buzz Lightyear

Buzz has stars in his eyes until Woody pulls him back down to Earth. For most of *Toy Story*, Buzz doesn't understand that he's a toy. But in *Toy Story 2*, he understands so well that he has to remind Woody. In *Toy Story 3*, Buzz is captured by a gang of hostile toys, who switch his setting to "demo." Woody and the others rescue him, but when they try to restore his setting, they accidentally switch his language button to Spanish!

STEP 1

STEP 2

STEP 3

iris is about 1/3 the size of the eye

YES!   NO!

brow should barely touch eye in normal pose; keep brows thick

the chin cleft is 1/2 the distance between lower lip and chin

basic head shape is rectangular; jaw drawn into bottom half of a hexagon

Buzz's chin takes up about 1/3 of his head

chin cleft looks like the number 9

eyes can change shape in exaggerated expressions

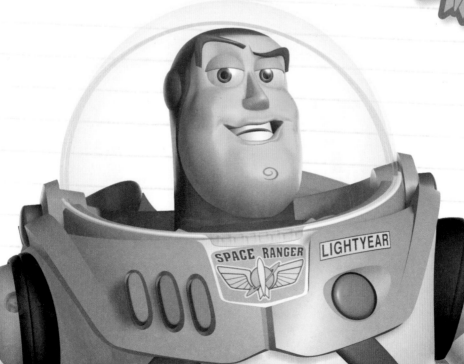

Lightning McQueen

Lightning McQueen is a worldwide celebrity whose every dream has come true. Famous, successful, and surrounded by great friends, Lightning is ready to enjoy time in the slow lane—just as soon as he wins the World Grand Prix.

Step 1

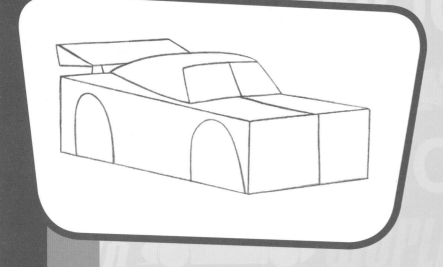

while he's competing in the races of the World Grand Prix, Lightning sports this tribute to Doc Hudson on his hood.

Step 2

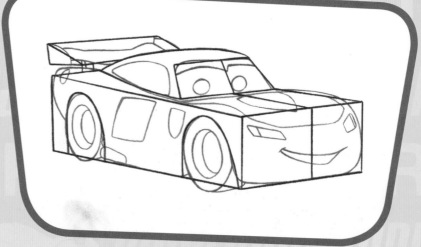

Step 3

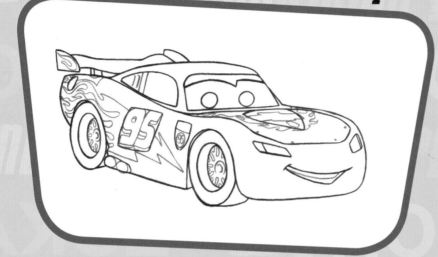

for the WGP races, Lightning gets a new, sportier spoiler!

Step 4

Mater

Mater is a friendly tow truck with a big heart, who is always willing to lend a helping hook. He is the self-proclaimed world's best backward driver. In Cars 2, Mater gets caught up in a world of espionage when he accompanies Lightning to the World Grand Prix.

Step 1

YES!
mirrors are at irregular angles

NO!
mirrors are not perfectly aligned

Step 2

keep facial expressions off center
to emphasize Mater's goofiness

YES!

YES!

NO!
too centered

Step 3

Step 4

YES!

NO!

his misshapen buckteeth aren't
perfect squares—and there's a
gap between them

WALL•E

WALL•E is a Waste Allocation Load Lifter—Earth class. Although considered a bit ancient for the twenty-ninth century, WALL•E is programmed with a strong directive: to collect and compact trash to clean up the overly polluted Earth. His boxy middle contains his compacting unit; his mechanical arms were designed to gather trash; and his triangular-shaped treads cover the wheels that help him maneuver over the rugged, trash-covered terrain.

YES!
eyes stay in
middle of face

NO!
they don't move
around on head

Step 1

Step 2

Step 4

Step 3

WALL·E's treads change shape when he moves

normal

high-speed

tip-toes

EVE

EVE is a probe-bot—an Extraterrestrial Vegetation Evaluator. That means she was programmed with the directive to find vegetation on Earth. If she finds a single plant on Earth, humans can return from their space travels and live on Earth again. A growing plant means the Earth's polluted environment can once again sustain life!

facial expressions

neutral

worried or sad

skeptical

laughing

Step 1

chest compartment can open

Step 2

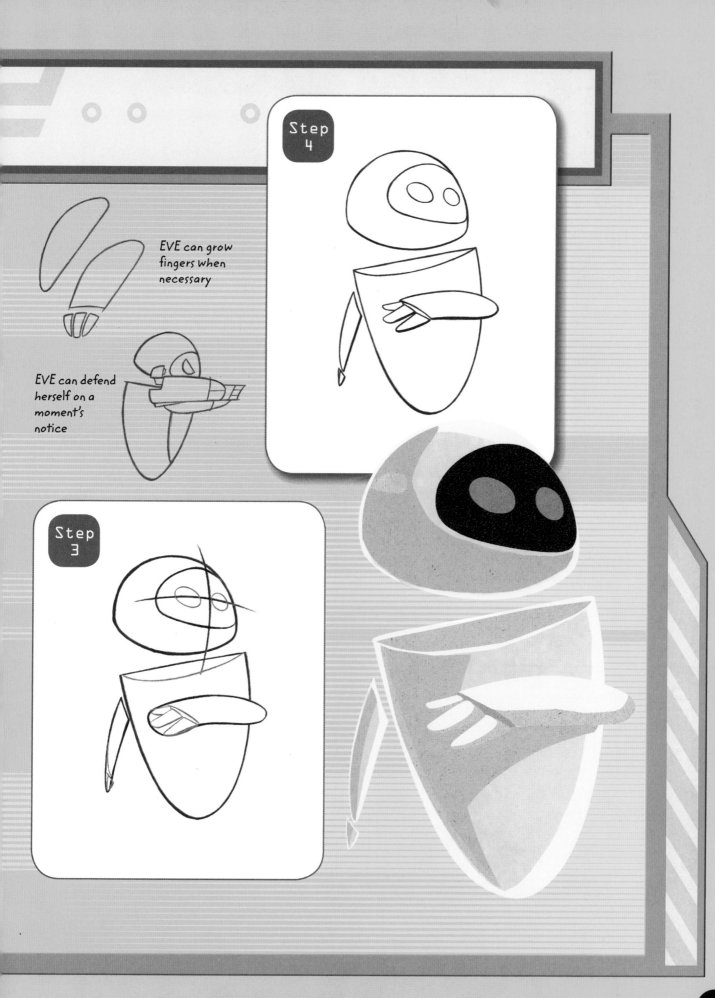

Step 4

Step 3

EVE can grow fingers when necessary

EVE can defend herself on a moment's notice

Nemo

Clownfish

Nemo is an adventurous little fish with a "lucky" fin who longs for excitement and friends to play with. But instead, he's saddled with Marlin, an overprotective single dad who never lets the poor little guy out of sight.

Well, one day, Nemo dares to show his friends he's not scared of the ocean (the way his dad is), and he swims off alone. He ends up getting a lot more excitement than he bargained for! But he also discovers just how brave and resourceful he can be.

from the side, Nemo is shaped like a Goldfish® cracker

from the front, body looks like a gumdrop

1

2

"lucky" fin is wedge-shaped with notch cut out

YES! rays follow curve of fin

NO! too straight and even

YES! varied stripe shapes

NO! too similar and too straight

YES! top (dorsal) fin is 2 different shapes pointing at different angles

NO! too even; too upright

Disney · PIXAR
FINDING NEMO

3

4

5

top fin is same height as 1 eye

Nemo is about 4 "eyes tall" including top fin

YES! bottom fins are set apart from each other

NO! fins don't look like a bow tie

41

DOry

Regal Blue Tang

Dory is one chatty, friendly, funny fish! She never gives up hope—when things get tough, she just keeps on swimming. Always willing and helpful, Dory has everything going for her except for one small thing—her memory. She can't remember anything! But she risks her own life to help Marlin find Nemo (despite the fact that she can't remember the little guy's name!).

from the front, Dory's stripe defines where her "eyebrows" end

freckles follow the curved bridge of her "nose"

YES! curved freckle pattern

NO! too straight

Dory is just over 4 times the size of Nemo

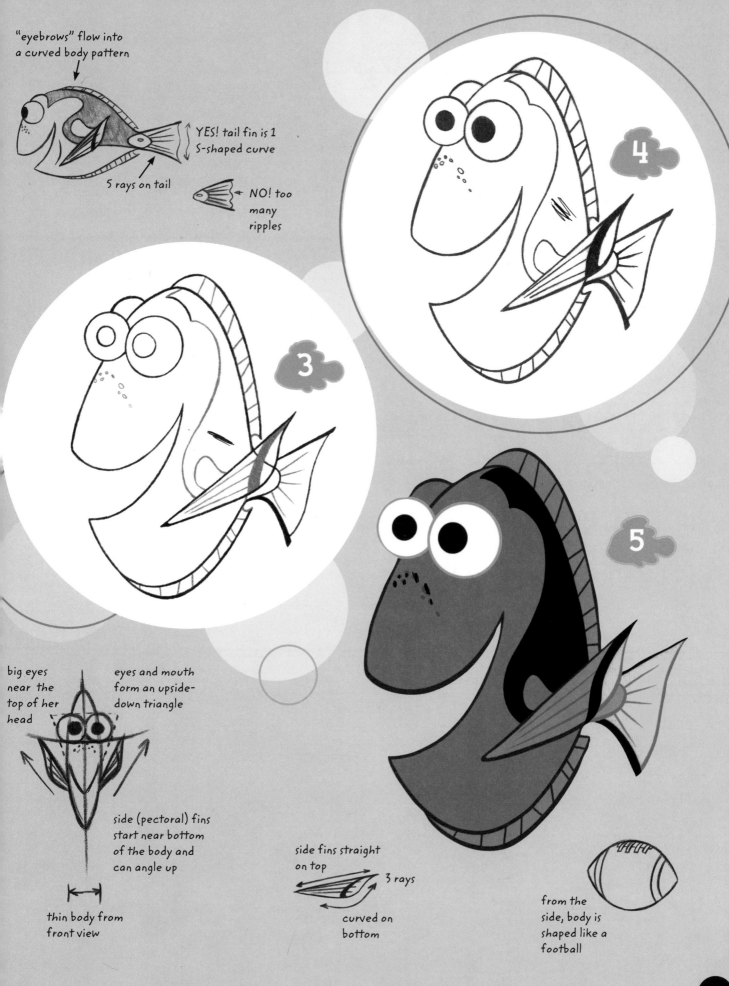

"eyebrows" flow into
a curved body pattern

YES! tail fin is 1
S-shaped curve

5 rays on tail

NO! too
many
ripples

3

4

5

big eyes
near the
top of her
head

eyes and mouth
form an upside-
down triangle

side (pectoral) fins
start near bottom
of the body and
can angle up

thin body from
front view

side fins straight
on top

3 rays

curved on
bottom

from the
side, body is
shaped like a
football

43

Sulley

"RRROAR!" Although Sulley scares kids for a living, he really has a heart of gold and is an all-around nice guy. Sulley's a gentle giant who would never hurt anyone—especially a kid! When he discovers that scaring them might not be the best thing for kids, he decides to do something about it, which changes Monsters, Inc., forever.

STEP 1

STEP 2

eyelid is rounded like this    YES!   NO!

YES! eyebrows overlap like this . . .

. . . and this

NO! not separated like this

outside of horn has angles; inside is curved

WE SCARE BECAUSE WE CARE

SULLEY

44

YES! bend knees to show weight

NO! don't make legs too straight

STEP 4

STEP 3

STEP 5

draw big hands with pointed nails

don't round out toes

YES!   NO!

Mike

Both best friend and scare assistant to James P. Sullivan, Mike Wazowski is proud of his job, and he loves the perks that go along with it. Mike wouldn't change a thing about his life—except maybe to eliminate all the paperwork he has to do. A little green ball of energy, Mike is always ready with a joke and a smile, especially for his best girl, Celia.

STEP 1

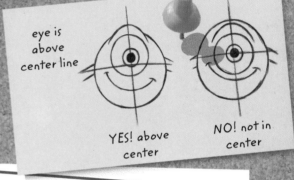

eye is above center line

YES! above center

NO! not in center

STEP 2

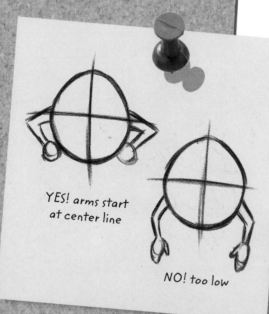

YES! arms start at center line

NO! too low

FOR YOUR SAFETY:
DO NOT FEED THE DISPATCHER

Boo

Don't be scared—Boo is just the name that Sulley gave to the little girl who journeyed through her closet door into Monstropolis. Adorable and extremely curious, Boo isn't afraid of Mike and Sulley—but they're plenty afraid of her! Completely unaware that she might be in danger, Boo is in no rush to go back to the human world; she's having too much fun in Monstropolis!

Powerful Screamer

STEP 1

YES! hands are small with short, round fingers

NO! not long and squared

YES! ear is on center line

NO! not too low

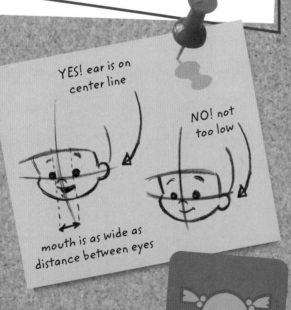

mouth is as wide as distance between eyes

STEP 2

STEP 3

YES! pigtails are rounded like this

NO! not straight like this

STEP 4

STEP 5

YES! big breaks in hair

NO! not little triangles

Boo

REMY

Remy is a little rat with big dreams. Born with a highly developed sense of smell, he can't stand eating garbage like the other rats, and he longs to become a gourmet chef. When Remy accidentally lands in the late, great Chef Auguste Gusteau's famous restaurant, Remy's dream just might come true . . . if he can remain hidden.

STEP 1

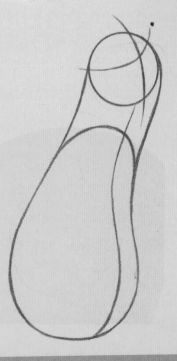

STEP 2

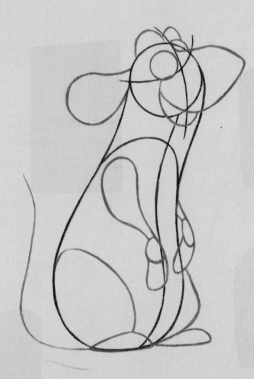

YES!
body leans
forward

NO!
doesn't tilt back-
ward

arm hair is
ragged and
loose

STEP 3

STEP 4

YES!
legs merge
with body
for a
relaxed look

NO!
legs are not
separate
shapes

LINGUINI & REMY

Linguini and Remy form an unusual partnership that takes them on harrowing adventures inside and out of Gusteau's restaurant. In the end, their hard work and strange working habits pay off deliciously!

STEP 1

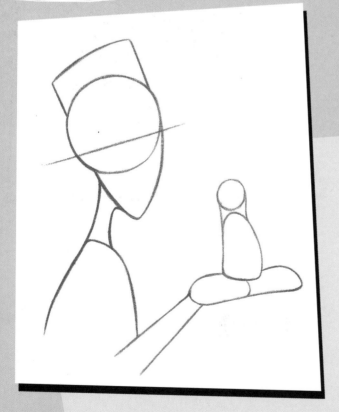

STEP 2

Linguini's head is shaped like an upside-down egg

Linguini's chef hat

Linguini's garbage boy hat

STEP 4

THE INCREDIBLES

MR. INCREDIBLE

A man of super strength, Mr. Incredible was once the best-known, most popular Super alive! Then, through the Super Relocation Program, Mr. Incredible became "normal" Bob Parr, a claims adjuster at probably the worst insurance company ever. But Bob is not content with his ordinary life. He misses being a Super. One day, a mysterious summons calls the hero back to action. . . .

STEP 1

STEP 2

YES!
mask is thick at
bridge of nose

NO!
mask doesn't taper
on bridge of nose

Bob has a very
large chin and
an arched nose

STEP 4

STEP 3

STEP 5

Head
shape

YES!
rounded
bottom

NO!
not straight

THE INCREDIBLES

Disney PRESENTS A PIXAR FILM

ELASTIGIRL

No one is as flexible as Elastigirl, a Super with an incredible reach! She could stretch her arm and land a punch before the crooks knew what hit them! But, as Helen Parr, Bob's wife and a mother of three, her Super powers are kept secret and largely unused—that is, until she finds out her Super spouse needs help! "Leave the saving of the world to the men? I don't think so!"

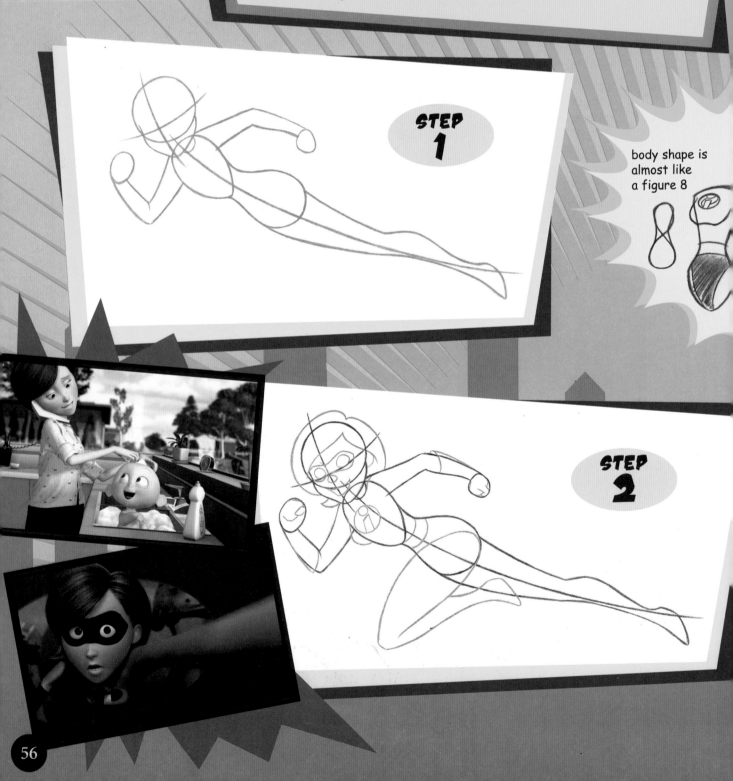

STEP 1

body shape is almost like a figure 8

STEP 2

STEP
3

keep
bridge of
nose short

YES!
short

NO!
not long

STEP
4

STEP
5

Helen's hair is
not completely
round—there
is a series of
flattened areas

FLAT
FLAT
FLAT

FROZONE

Frozone was once known as the coolest Super on the planet. With the ability to create ice from the moisture in the air, he could build ice bridges, skate across them with special boots, and freeze criminals right in their tracks. Known as Lucius Best in his secret life, Frozone is also Mr. Incredible's best friend— and a reluctant partner in Bob's undercover heroics.

STEP 3

STEP 4

STEP 5

Frozone's head is shaped like a cold capsule

ice rays come from hands

YES!
nose is round on top with point at nostril

NO!
nose not pointed at top and round at bottom

59

Flik

Flik is a lovable worker ant whose inventions are often brilliant but disastrous. Clumsy and easily excited, Flik is known for his uncanny ability to make things go wrong. But his ideas are what ultimately save the ant colony from Hopper and his gang.

The 2 parts of Flik's antennae form a right angle

NO!

YES!

The first antenna segments are like tapered straws

With antennae, he's about 5 heads tall

step 1

Flik has 3 toes

Flik's torso is like a bowling pin

His abdomen is like a bowling ball

step 2

Expressions

Sheepish

Choked up

Dismayed

A The pose is worked out with a stick figure

The ants have 4 digits on each hand: 3 fingers and 1 thumb

Flik's arms look like sleeves

Flik's antennae are composed of 2 nearly straight segments

B Then basic shapes are built up

A bit of eyelid usually shows

step 3

His top teeth show when he smiles

When Flik smiles, his cheek comes over the eye

C Finally the details are added

D Back to the drawing board!

Atta

Atta is the stressed-out princess who is in training to become leader of the ant colony. She has the makings of a good queen, but she's still learning. Flik often flusters her with his unconventionality, but there is something in the back of Atta's mind that tells her that Flik and his ideas are worthy of consideration.

Atta's eyes are elliptical

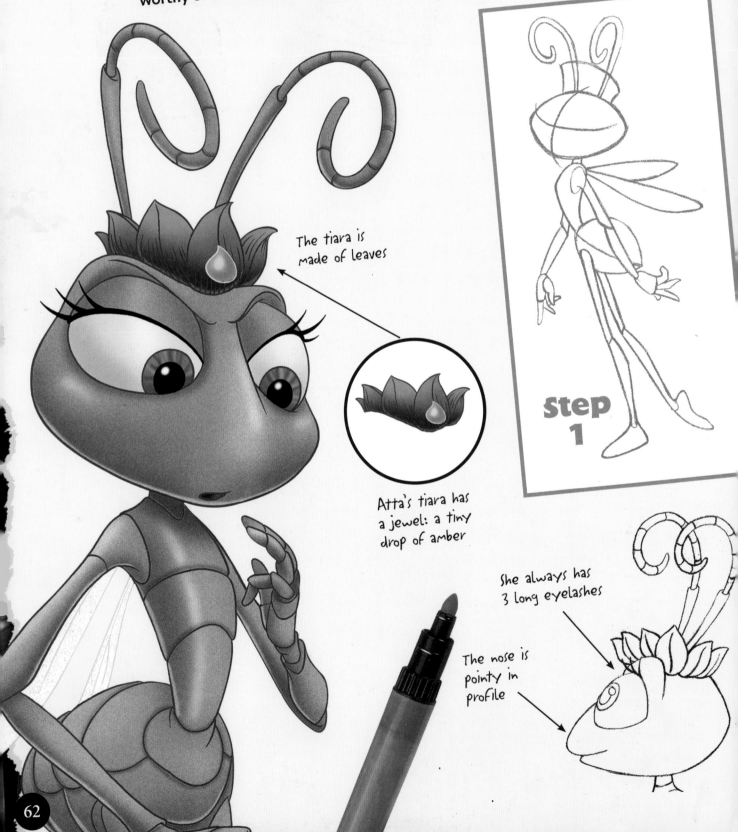

The tiara is made of leaves

Atta's tiara has a jewel: a tiny drop of amber

Step 1

She always has 3 long eyelashes

The nose is pointy in profile

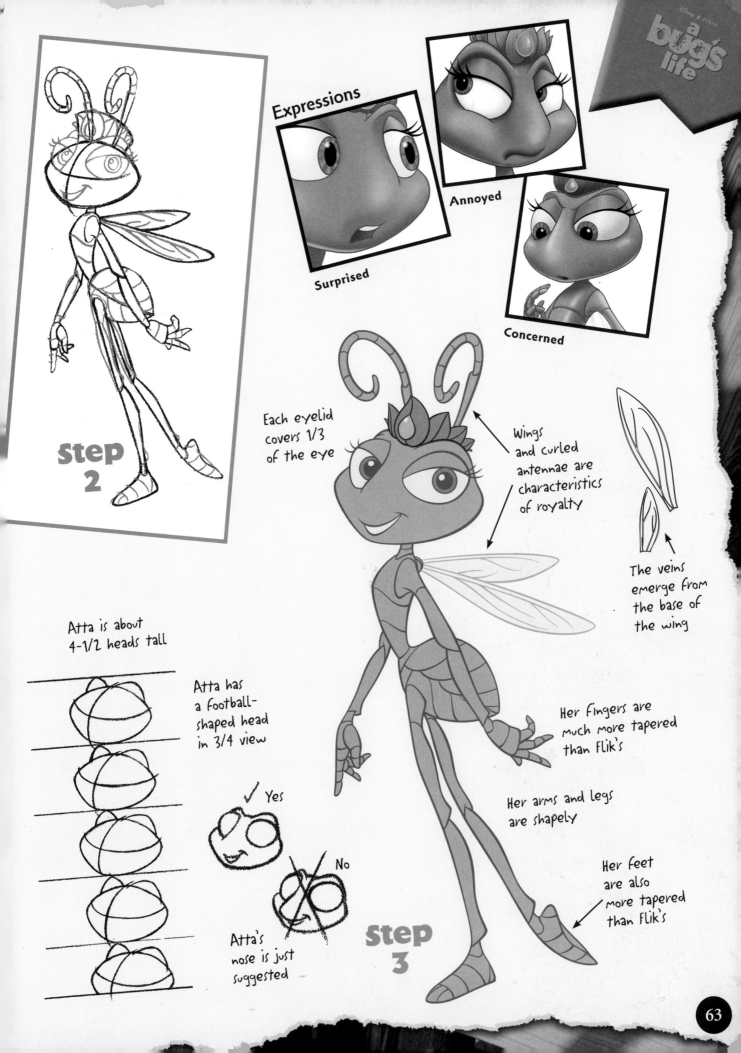

Expressions

Surprised

Annoyed

Concerned

step 2

Each eyelid covers 1/3 of the eye

Wings and curled antennae are characteristics of royalty

The veins emerge from the base of the wing

Atta is about 4-1/2 heads tall

Atta has a football-shaped head in 3/4 view

✓ Yes

No

Atta's nose is just suggested

step 3

Her fingers are much more tapered than Flik's

Her arms and legs are shapely

Her feet are also more tapered than Flik's

63

The End

Now that you've learned how to draw your favorite
Disney · Pixar characters, try experimenting on your own.
All you need is your paper, pencil, and plenty of imagination!